Who
Has Max?

by Tanner Gay
illustrations by Holly Cooper

Harcourt Brace & Company

Orlando   Atlanta   Austin   Boston   San Francisco   Chicago   Dallas   New York   Toronto   London

The whole family was going to Big Tan Gap. Dad had to pack the van.

"Max has a bag," said Jan.
"Thanks, Max," said Dad, as
he packed the bag on the rack.

Max helped Sam with the map and the hats.

"Thanks, Max," said Sam.

Mother had ham and other things to eat.

"No, Max! Not you!" Mother laughed. "*I'll* pack the ham."

At last they sat down in
the van. "Who has our hats?"
asked Dad.

"We do," said Jan and Sam.

"Who has the map?" asked Dad.

"I do," said Mother.

"Good," said Dad. "We can
get some gas and go." He
started to back the van out.

Then Mother asked, "Who has Max?"

They looked in the back of
the van, where Max always sat.
Max wasn't there.

"I thought YOU had Max!"
Jan said to Sam.
"I thought YOU had Max!"
Sam said to Jan.

They ran back into the house.
Max sat on his mat, looking
very sad!

"Max!" said Jan. "We feel so bad, after all you did to help! Come on. You are going, too!"

Back in the van, Jan gave
Max a pat. "Sit on my lap and
have a nap," she said.

So Max had a nap on Jan's lap—all the way to Big Tan Gap.

The whole family had a great time at Big Tan Gap. Max had the best time of all!